D0514558

Poetry Patterns

Your students *can* write poetry! The 40-plus lessons in
Poetry Patterns provide step-by-step guidance for writing
a rich variety of rhyming and nonrhyming poetry forms—
from the usual (Couplets, Haiku) to the exotic (Sneaky poetry,
Inside-Outside poetry).

The variety of poetry forms and
topics in *Poetry Patterns*

- provides something of interest
  for all students,

- encourages students to write
  about a broad range of
  experiences and feelings, and

- provides opportunities for
  students at all levels
  of writing experience.

Acknowledgment
The original edition of Poetry Patterns *was conceptualized and written by
Eleanor Orndorf. The samples of student poetry included in the original edition
and in this revision were written by fifth-grade students of the Norris School
District in Bakersfield, California.*

EMC 733

Evan-Moor®
EDUCATIONAL PUBLISHERS
Helping Children Learn since 1979

Author: Original Edition–Eleanor Orndorf
            Revised–Jo Ellen Moore
Editor: Marilyn Evans
Designer: Keli Winters
Illustrators: Jo Larsen
            Don Robison
Cover: Cheryl Puckett

**Congratulations on your purchase of some of the
finest teaching materials in the world.**

For information about other Evan-Moor products,
call 1-800-777-4362 or FAX 1-800-777-4332.
Visit our Web site www.evan-moor.com
for additional product information.

Contents

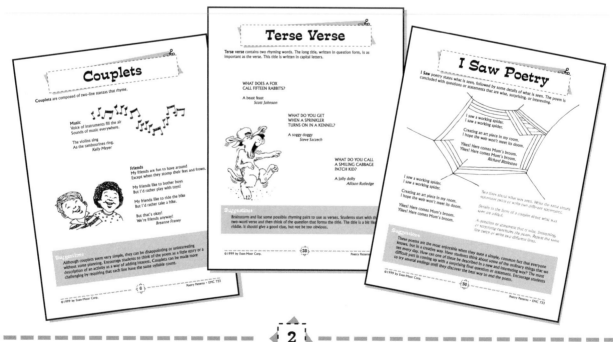

©1999 by Evan-Moor Corp.

Poetry Patterns • EMC 733

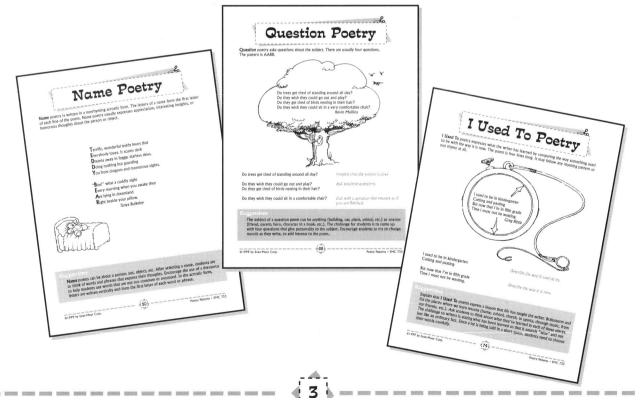

Poetry Patterns • EMC 733

Using *Poetry Patterns*

Lesson Format

The lessons in *Poetry Patterns* have two components:
- The first page describes the poetry form and may explain the pattern, shows one or more student-written examples, and gives suggestions for conducting the lesson.
- The second page is a reproducible student work form. Steps are given to guide the student through the writing process for that poetry pattern. Many pages also provide an area where the completed poem can be written.

Plan the Lesson

- Decide which form of poetry you would like your students to learn to write.
  Some easier forms: couplet, word-count cinquain, free verse, terse verse
  Some harder forms: ballad, diamonte, syllable-count cinquain, I Wish poetry
- Make an overhead transparency of the sample poem.
- Reproduce the student work form if students will be working independently.

Prewriting

- Discuss the description of the poetry form given at the top of the transparency.
- Read the sample poem(s) with students.
- Go through the poem step by step to see how the pattern has been followed.

Writing

Guided: If the poetry pattern is new to students, write the poem together. (See the sample lesson on page 5.)

Independent: Students follow the poetry form using the reproducible work form as a guide.

Sharing and Publishing

Provide opportunities for students to share their poems with others. This modeling will motivate continued writing and be especially helpful for hesitant writers. (See pages 92–95 for suggestions.)

A Sample Lesson

This sample lesson using haiku models how a poetry pattern might be taught.

Prewriting

Read samples of haiku.
Show the overhead transparency of page 34.
Read the samples together and discuss the haiku pattern.
Have students count to see how well each sample fits the
5-7-5 syllable count.
Discuss the feeling or the word picture expressed by the
poem. Talk about how the language used helps to express
a feeling or paint a picture.

Writing

As a class, select a topic. (Remind students that haiku usually relates to nature in some way.)

firefly

Brainstorm and list words and phrases that describe the topic.

tiny	flies around at dusk	twinkling tail light
small	flies in the night sky	flashing off and on
little	swooping here and there	shining like a lantern
wee	dancing in the dark	like little stars in my backyard
mysterious	quietly moving	sending messages with its light

Students select from the list to create a sentence about the topic. They organize the words
into three interesting phrases. This is a time to change, rearrange, add, or omit words to make
the phrases more interesting.

Tiny firefly in the dark like little stars dancing in my backyard.
Mysterious insect moves in the night sending messages with its light.

Finally, students work with the words in each phrase to reach the required syllable count. This
may mean changing, adding, or omitting words.

Magical insect
sends messages with its light—
firefly in the night.

Students copy and illustrate the finished poem.

Couplets

Couplets are composed of two-line stanzas that rhyme.

Title → **Music**

Stanza { Voice of instruments fill the air
Sounds of music everywhere.

Stanza { The violins sing
As the tambourines ring.
Kelly Meyer

Friends
My friends are fun to have around
Except when they stomp their feet and frown.

My friends like to bother boys
But I'd rather play with toys!

My friends like to ride the bike
But I'd rather take a hike.

But that's okay!
We're friends anyway!
Breanne Franey

Suggestions

Although couplets seem very simple, they can be disappointing or uninteresting without some planning. Encourage students to think of the poem as a little story or a description of an activity as a way of adding interest. Couplets can be made more challenging by requiring that each line have the same syllable count.

A **couplet** is composed of two-line stanzas that rhyme.

1 Select a subject. _____

2 Write a first line about the subject.

_____

List words that rhyme with the last word in the first line.

_____   _____   _____

_____   _____   _____

_____   _____   _____

3 Write a second line ending with a rhyming word from your list.

_____

4 Follow the same steps if you want to write other couplets about your topic. Try to write at least two couplets about your subject.

Copy and illustrate your poem here.

- -

_____
                                                title
        by_____

_____

_____

_____

_____

_____

_____

                    Poetry Patterns • EMC 733

Giving Poetry

Giving poetry names a subject that gives an interesting or unusual gift.

Swimming pools
give cool refreshment
to hot bodies
on scorching, summer days.
Katie Meyer

Swimming pools	*State the subject. You may add an adjective describing it.*
give cool refreshment	*Describe what the subject "gives."*
to hot bodies	*Who or what is receiving the gift? Describe it.*
on scorching, summer days.	*Describe when it happens. Use at least two interesting adjectives.*

Suggestions

Encourage students to think of gifts they receive from everyday objects or from common places. Think of adjectives that are opposites to use in lines 2 and 3. This is a good time to practice using a thesaurus to find antonyms.

 Poetry Patterns • EMC 733

Name

> **Giving** poetry names and describes a subject
> that gives an interesting or unusual gift.

1 Choose a subject. List several words that describe it. Circle the word you like best.

_____   _____   _____

_____   _____   _____

_____   _____   _____

2 Write several phrases that describe what the subject "gives." Circle the phrase you like best.

_____   _____

_____   _____

3 Write phrases telling who or what is receiving the gift. (The idea of this line should be the opposite of line 2.) Circle the phrase you like best.

_____   _____

_____   _____

4 Describe when it happens. Use at least two interesting adjectives. Circle the phrase you like best.

_____   _____

_____   _____

5 Use the circled phrases to write your poem on another sheet of paper. Change, add, or remove words to make the giving poem more interesting.

6 Copy and illustrate the completed poem.

Change Poetry

Change poetry tells of three or more stages that occur as a thing evolves into something new. Each stage is a step in that evolution. Finally, a thoughtful statement is made about the changes. The poem follows an ABCB pattern.

Seed into sapling,
sapling into tree,
I really see "Home, Sweet Home"
right in front of me.
Megan Fowler

Seed into sapling,
sapling into tree,

I really see "Home, Sweet Home"
right in front of me.

The three stages are stated here. Notice the changes in the first two lines.

A thoughtful statement follows the stages. The final line should rhyme with line 2.

Suggestions

Prepare students for this writing project by asking them to think of several sets of subjects with three stages: eggs, tadpoles, frogs; baby, child, adult; arguing, fighting, war. The final sentence of a change poem is very important to its meaning. Encourage students to try to find a phrase that captures both understanding and an emotion. Use the sample poem as an example. What words show an understanding of what happens in the last stage? (the construction of a home) How was it expressed to evoke emotion? ("Home, Sweet Home" is a phrase often used to express the warmth and love existing in one's home.)

Change poetry tells of three or more stages
that occur as a thing evolves into something new.
The poem follows an ABCB pattern.

1 Think of something that changes in at least three ways. List the three changes here.

_____   _____   _____

2 Write two lines describing the first two changes.

_____

_____

3 Write about the final change. End with a thoughtful statement about what has happened. The last line should rhyme with line 2.

_____

_____

Copy and illustrate your poem here.

_____
title

by_____

_____

_____

_____

_____

Animal Prayer Poetry

Animal Prayer poetry is written from the animal's point of view. It is usually a request stated in a descriptive and colorful manner.

Prayer of the Deer
In this deep forest
of freedom and peace
I must pray for protection
from growling bears
and two-legged beasts.
Mel Gragirena

Prayer of the Deer	*The animal is identified in the title or first line.*
In this deep forest of freedom and peace	*A description of its habitat follows.*
I must pray for protection from growling bears and two-legged beasts.	*A request or statement is made.*

Suggestions

Spend time brainstorming the types of things an animal might request and how these requests might be stated. After students have written a first draft, encourage them to look closely at each word they've used. Could the word be exchanged for a more accurate, interesting, or picturesque word? Could another adjective or adverb be added to add action to the poem? Could a word be removed to make the language more poetic?

> **Animal Prayer** poetry is a request made by an animal.

1 Select an animal. List things the animal might pray for. Circle the idea you like best.

_____   _____

_____   _____

2 Write a title identifying the animal. Or write a first line that names and describes the animal.

_____

3 Write a description of the animal's habitat. This may be one or more lines.

_____

_____

4 Write a request or statement about what the animal wants. This may be one or more lines.

_____

_____

5 Think about what you have written. How can you make it better? Do you need to change, add, or remove a word?

Copy and illustrate your poem here.

_____

_____
title

by_____

_____

_____

_____

_____

_____

Onomatopoeia

Onomatopoeia is poetry in which words are used to make sounds.

It's the Witch
Listen! Listen!
do you hear
something queer
something that goes
slish
slosh
slash
slish
slosh
slash
do you hear?
It's It's
It's It's
WITCH! WITCH!
Sloshing in the rain
with her crooked cane
her face
olive green!!!
and then I heard a
S C R E A M !
he ha he he
It's the
W I T C H
Cara Taylor

Onomatopoeia is poetry in which words are used to make sounds.

1 Think of a subject for your poem. It should be something that involves a lot of different sounds.

_____

2 List sounds you might use in your poem.

_____ _____ _____

_____ _____ _____

_____ _____ _____

3 Write your basic poem here. It should tell a little story, tell about an event, or describe your subject. Leave spaces where you think you will put sound words. You might try to have a few lines that rhyme, but rhyming isn't necessary.

_____

_____

_____

_____

_____

_____

4 Decide which sounds to use and where the sounds will go in the poem. Fit these into your basic poem.

5 Move words around until the poem sounds just right.

6 Copy and illustrate your poem.

Poetry Patterns • EMC 733

Thanksgiving Poetry

Thanksgiving poetry challenges students to record their feelings in a beautiful and inspiring way in 12 lines. It may be written as an expression of thankfulness or as a prayer.

Thou art Lord. I thank thee for my
House and my life and
Also for my friends
Near and far.
Know that I am thankful for
Shoes on my feet and food in my stomach, for
Great stars in the skies.
I love flowers with their
Vibrant rainbow of colors.
I am thankful for living in a
Nation that is free.
God, I thank thee for everything thou hast given me. Amen.
Julie McAfee

Suggestions

Brainstorm and list things students are thankful for. Encourage them to express a thought which is begun and finished in the twelve lines. If it is a prayer, students should try to arrive at a conclusion. If it is an expression of thanks for country, family, health, etc., they should try to make the last words create a feeling that the poem has been finished.

Students can create an old-fashioned sounding poem by using Old English words such as thou, thee (you), art (are), hath (have), maketh (makes), etc.

Poetry Patterns • EMC 733

Thanksgiving poetry tells what you are thankful for. Each
line begins with one of the letters in the word "Thanksgiving."

1 Make a list of things you are thankful for.

_____   _____

_____   _____

_____   _____

_____   _____

2 Use the items in your list as you write. Arrange the sentences so that each line begins with
a letter in the word "Thanksgiving."

T _____

H _____

A _____

N _____

K _____

S _____

G _____

I _____

V _____

I _____

N _____

G _____

3 Copy and illustrate your poem.

Poetry Patterns • EMC 733

Months Poetry

Months poetry is a series of couplets about the months of the year. Each couplet describes the month or tells something about it.

January, the month with lots of snow.
It's fun for everyone, you know.

February, the month with Valentine's Day.
I will send a card and candy your way.

March is when my mom will be thirty-five.
What a fun month to be alive.

April, the month with April Fools' Day.
And everybody likes it that way.

May is when the flowers burst out.
When we can laugh, and play, and shout.

June is when we get out of school.
When we can go home and swim in the pool.

In July my brother will be thirteen.
We celebrate it with cake and ice cream.

In August I can laugh, and play
football and basketball during the day.

I have my birthday in September.
I never forget, I always remember.

October is spooky costumes on Halloween.
With fun and games, and scary screams.

In November there is Thanksgiving Day.
On the table the turkey will lay.

In December we celebrate Christmas.
It's the best time of year for all of us.

Ben Affleck

Suggestions

Months poetry offers a wide range of topics on which students can write. It can be personalized to fit family holidays and celebrations. It can be historical, utilizing interesting information found during research. It can be described in colors or moods or changes in nature.

Encourage students to pay close attention as they edit their rough drafts, choosing the most expressive phrases and eliminating unnecessary words.

Poetry Patterns • EMC 733

Months poetry is written in couplets and
describes or tells about each month of the year.

Select a theme for your poem (family events, holidays, weather, fun, etc.). Write one couplet for
each month.

January _____

_____

February _____

_____

March _____

_____

April _____

_____

May _____

_____

June _____

_____

July _____

_____

Poetry Patterns • EMC 733

August _____

_____

September _____

_____

October _____

_____

November _____

_____

December _____

_____

Copy your poem. Make an interesting border around it.

Cinquain

A **cinquain** is a five-line poem. The traditional cinquain follows a syllable count, with lines of 2 syllables, 4 syllables, 6 syllables, 8 syllables, 2 syllables. A simpler version follows the "word" pattern given below.

Trumpet
Golden, gleaming
Puckering, puffing, blowing
Mean machine
Bronze flower
　　　　Joel Griffin

Trumpet	*Write a one-word subject.*
Golden, gleaming	*Use two adjectives to describe it.*
Puckering, puffing, blowing	*Write three very descriptive action words.*
Mean machine	*Make a short statement about the subject.*
Bronze flower	*End with a synonym filled with imagination.*

Suggestions

Selecting words for a cinquain can be challenging, especially when using the syllable form. Encourage students to use a thesaurus to find words that express precisely what is being described. The last line is very important and can be difficult. Students should strive to choose a word that gives a little "twist" or extra "punch" to the end of the verse.

　　　　　　Poetry Patterns • EMC 733

A **cinquain** is a five-line poem describing a subject. This version follows a word pattern.

Write a "word" cinquain following these directions:

1 Write a one-word subject. _____

2 Use two adjectives to describe the subject.

_____

3 Write three descriptive action words about the subject.

_____

4 Make a short statement about the subject. (This is usually a four-word phrase.)

_____

5 End with a synonym for the subject. (This is usually one word.)

_____

Copy and illustrate your poem here.

_____

_____

_____

_____

by _____

©1999 by Evan-Moor Corp.   Poetry Patterns • EMC 733

A **cinquain** is a five-line poem describing a subject.
This traditional pattern follows a syllable count.

Write a "syllable-count" cinquain here.

1 Write a 2-syllable title. _____

2 Write a 4-syllable word or phrase about the title.

_____

3 Write a 6-syllable phrase about the title.

_____

4 Write an 8-syllable phrase about the title.

_____

5 Write a 2-syllable word that refers to the title.

_____

Copy and illustrate your poem here.

_____

_____

_____

_____

_____

by _____

Ballad Poetry

Ballads are simple stories told in poetic form. Sometimes a lesson is told in the last phrase. A ballad can have any number of stanzas, and generally follows an ABCB pattern. Ballads are used as verses of songs. Much country music is simply a ballad that is sung.

The Challenger

In the year of 1986
The Challenger went up into space.
On board were astronauts and a teacher
Trying to find an unexplored place.

Make a when, what, and where statement. Add more information.

The audience roared and were filled with hope.
And finally the moment was here.
The fans watched in awe...
While it blew up, and they were full of fear.

Continue the story.

The teacher and six astronauts
In a moment...They were gone.
But they are up in space,
At home, where they belong.
                    Sarah Moore

Finish the story with a thoughtful ending.

Suggestions

Brainstorm with students to list possible topics. These can come from history, current events, or students' own lives. Remind students to select a story to tell that has quite a lot of emotion in it. Ballads are full of feeling often stemming from sad or tragic events. There should be a smooth story with interesting details and a very definite ending. Have students rewrite their ballad until it flows like a song that is being spoken.

Poetry Patterns • EMC 733

A **ballad** tells a simple story in poetry form. It usually follows the ABCB rhyming pattern. It can have any number of stanzas. Sometimes a lesson is stated in the last stanza.

1 Think of an event.
Write down the information you know about the event. When did it happen? What happened? Where did it happen? You may need to do some research to find more information.

_____

_____

_____

_____

_____

_____

_____

_____

_____

_____

_____

2 Use the information to write the first draft of a ballad.
    a. Make a when, what, and where statement, and then add more information about what is happening. Arrange the information in a rhyming pattern (ABCB).

    b. Continue the story in rhyme describing what happens next. This can be one or more stanzas. Use as many as you need to tell your story.

    c. Describe how the story ends. Finish the stanza with a thoughtful line to end your ballad.

3 Copy and illustrate your ballad.

                                 Poetry Patterns • EMC 733

Free Verse

Free verse expresses an idea, a story, or a feeling in a rhythmic form. It has no particular pattern, and may or may not have rhyming phrases.

Daybreak
Alarm rings
Mom enters
Sadness comes
I must get up
Joel Walton

In the hustle
and bustle
of a big busy city
I look up and say
Why is it like this?
Am I the only one who cares
Except for the "Big Guy" up there?
Jay Heisey

Suggestions

Students begin by thinking of possible subjects for free verse. Ask:
   What are you interested in?
   What makes you happy, sad, or angry?
   What ideas do you have about the future?
   What was an especially good time in your life?
   What was an especially bad time in your life?
The answers to any of these questions can provide material for free verse.

A careful choice of words and phrases, arranged in an interesting manner, are necessary to create a verse that flows in a poetic way.

Free verse doesn't have a specific pattern. In free verse it is the rhythm and the language used to express an idea that makes the poem.

1 Think about things you are interested in, what you are happy or sad about, and what you are concerned about. Choose a subject. It can be an idea, an impression, or a story. List your thoughts about the subject.

_____

_____

_____

_____

_____

2 Select the thoughts you like best from your list and arrange them in a poetic way. Keep working with the words and their arrangement until you are satisfied with the sound of the verse.

_____

_____

_____

_____

_____

_____

3 Copy and illustrate your poem.

Terse Verse

Terse verse contains two rhyming words. The long title, written in question form, is as important as the verse. This title is written in capital letters.

WHAT DOES A FOX
CALL FIFTEEN RABBITS?

A beast feast
Scott Johnson

WHAT DO YOU GET
WHEN A SPRINKLER
TURNS ON IN A KENNEL?

A soggy doggy
Steve Szczech

WHAT DO YOU CALL
A SMILING CABBAGE
PATCH KID?

A jolly dolly
Allison Rutledge

Suggestions

Brainstorm and list some possible rhyming pairs to use as verses. Students start with the two-word verse and then think of the question that forms the title. The title is a bit like a riddle. It should give a good clue, but not be too obvious.

Terse verse contains two rhyming words.
The title is a question about the verse.
It is written in capital letters.

1 List pairs of interesting rhyming words.

_____   _____

_____   _____

_____   _____

2 Select a rhyming pair. Think of a question about the rhyming words. The title is like a riddle. Give a good clue, but don't give away the answer. You may want to write questions for several rhyming pairs. Pick the one you like best.

_____

_____

_____

_____

Copy and illustrate your poem here. Write the title question in capital letters.
Write the poem after the word "A."

- -

WHAT _____

_____
                                title
A _____

                    by _____

Poetry Patterns • EMC 733

Snowman Poetry

Snowman poetry is written in two stanzas. The first stanza asks questions. The second stanza contains the answers.

Snowman on the ground
Why is it that you frown?
Why do you look so sad?
Can't you look a little glad?

Oh, my friend
My mouth will not bend.
I was made this way by a child.
Could you give me a smile?
Chet Johns

Snowman on the ground

The snowman is named and the location stated.

Why is it that you frown?
Why do you look so sad?
Can't you look a little glad?

The questions are asked.
They should be related.

Oh, my friend

The questioner is identified.

My mouth will not bend.
I was made this way by a child.
Could you give me a smile?

The answer is given.

Suggestions

Explain that the rhyming pattern can be changed or the poem can be written as free verse. However, it must retain the question and answer format. (The sample is written in an AABB quatrain form.) Have the class brainstorm and list questions that might be asked of a snowman and possible answers the snowman might give.

Students can use this type of verse to "question" anyone or anything. For example, a scarecrow, a wooden soldier, a gingerbread man, the man in the moon, a house, a broom, etc., would all be good topics.

> **Snowman** poetry is written in two stanzas. The first stanza asks questions. The second stanza contains the answers.

1 First stanza: Name the snowman and give its location.

_____

2 Ask two or more related questions.

_____

_____

_____

Second stanza: Identify the questioner.

_____

3 Give the answer.

_____

_____

_____

Copy and illustrate your poem here.

- -

_____
title

by _____

_____

_____

_____

_____

_____

_____

_____

Poetry Patterns • EMC 733

Diamonte Poetry

Diamonte poetry shows change. The beginning line and the last line are opposites or contrasting words. The poem shows a gradual change from the first line to the last line. It is written in the shape of a diamond.

War
run, hit
stabbing, shooting, killing
Vietnam, Iran, United States, Japan
living, relaxing, singing
harmony, free
Peace
Ryan Young

Tears
ache, grief
wept, sobbed, mourned
drops, water, pleasure, grin
celebrated, laughed, cheered
delight, joy
Smiles
Jo Ellen Moore

Tears	*State a noun that is the opposite of the noun in the last line.*
ache, grief	*Write two words describing the noun in line 1.*
wept, sobbed, mourned	Write three verbs related to the noun in line 1. End the words with "ing" or "ed."
drops, water, pleasure, grin	*Write two nouns that relate to line 1 followed by two nouns that relate to line 7.*
celebrated, laughed, cheered	*Write three verbs related to the noun in line 7. End the words with "ing" or "ed."*
delight, joy	*Write two words describing the noun in line 7.*
Smiles	Write the noun that is opposite of the noun on line 1.

Suggestions

Brainstorm and list interesting and powerful words. Then list their opposites. Students choose a pair of opposites for the first line and the last line of the poem. They then work on the words needed to fill in the remaining lines. Words should be organized so they flow from one to another in a way that makes sense. Encourage students to use a dictionary or thesaurus to find just the right words.

Diamonte poetry shows a change slowly occurring from the first line to the last line. It is written in the shape of a diamond.

Line 1 and Line 7

Think of two interesting words that are opposites. Write one on the first line and one on the last line of the form at the bottom of the page.

Line 2

Think of words that describe the noun in line 1. Pick the two you like best to write on the second line of the form.

Line 3

Think of verbs relating to the noun in line 1. End the words with "ing" or "ed." Pick the three you like best to write on the third line of the form.

Line 4

Think of two nouns that relate to line 1 and two nouns that relate to line 7 of your poem. Write them on the fourth line of the form.

Line 5

Think of three verbs relating to the noun in line 7. End the words with "ing" or "ed." Write them on the fifth line of the form.

Line 6

Think of two words that describe the noun in line 7. Write them on the sixth line of the form.

_____

_____

_____

_____

_____

_____

_____

by _____

Copy and illustrate your poem.

Poetry Patterns • EMC 733

Haiku

Haiku is a single thought expressed in three nonrhyming lines. The first line has 5 syllables, the second line has 7 syllables, and the third line has 5 syllables.

Sweet smells fill the air
Flowers blooming everywhere
Babes born here and there.
Ashley Daniel

My ship floats the sea
I'll drift to some distant place.
Better get started!
Justin Warwick

Brisk spring and fall air
New colors glance in my hair
As I watch in awe.
Tracie Fowler

Brisk spring and fall air	*5 syllables*
New colors glance in my hair	*7 syllables*
As I watch in awe.	*5 syllables*

Suggestions

Haiku very often describes subjects from nature. Brainstorm and list the types of subjects writers might choose.

Students start with a thought about a single topic. This can be written in the form of a sentence or as phrases. They then work with the words to create the correct syllable count for each of the three lines.

Haiku is one thought expressed in three lines that do not rhyme.
Line 1—5 syllables; Line 2—7 syllables; Line 3—5 syllables.

1 Think of a subject. Write a sentence or several phrases about it.

_____

_____

_____

_____

2 Arrange the sentence or phrases to fit the haiku pattern.

5 syllables _____

7 syllables _____

5 syllables _____

Copy and illustrate your poem here.

_____

_____

_____

by _____

Poetry Patterns • EMC 733

I Saw Poetry

I Saw poetry states what is seen, followed by some details of what is seen. The poem is concluded with questions or statements that are wise, surprising, or interesting.

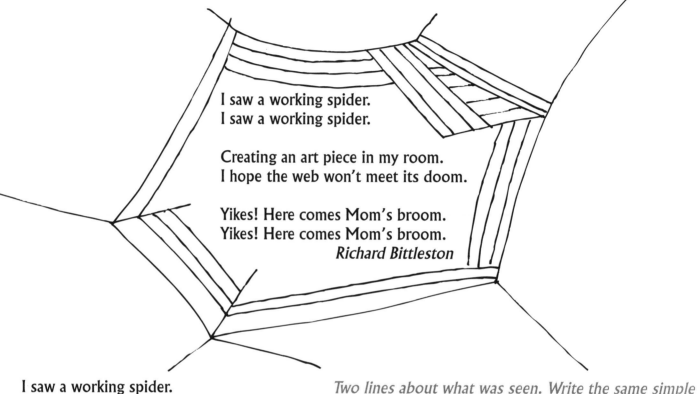

I saw a working spider.
I saw a working spider.

Creating an art piece in my room.
I hope the web won't meet its doom.

Yikes! Here comes Mom's broom.
Yikes! Here comes Mom's broom.
Richard Bittleston

I saw a working spider.
I saw a working spider.

Two lines about what was seen. Write the same simple statement twice or write two different statements.

Creating an art piece in my room.
I hope the web won't meet its doom.

Details in the form of a couplet about what was seen are added.

Yikes! Here comes Mom's broom.
Yikes! Here comes Mom's broom.

A question or statement that is wise, interesting, or surprising concludes the poem. Repeat the same line twice or write two different lines.

Suggestions

These poems are the most enjoyable when they state a simple, common fact that everyone knows, but in a creative way. Have students think about some of the ordinary things that we see every day. How can one of these be described in a new and interesting way? The most difficult part is coming up with a surprising final question or statement. Encourage students to try several endings until they discover the best way to end the poem.

36

© 1999 by Evan-Moor Corp.
Poetry Patterns • EMC 733

> **I Saw** poetry describes something that is seen. The poem
> ends with a wise, surprising, or interesting question or statement.

1 Choose a subject to write about. Write a phrase naming what you see. Repeat the phrase or write a second phrase that names what is seen in a new way.

_____

_____

2 Write a rhyming couplet giving some details about what you see.

_____

_____

3 End the poem with a question or statement that is wise, interesting, or surprising. Repeat the line twice or write two different lines.

_____

_____

Copy and illustrate your poem here.

_____
title

by _____

_____

_____

_____

_____

_____

_____

Poetry Patterns • EMC 733

This Is Mine Poetry

This Is Mine poetry names and describes a possession. It is written in quatrains with an ABCB pattern. The last stanza concludes the poem in a humorous or surprising way.

These are my sneakers
They're both exactly the same
They are old
And very lame.

These are my sneakers
All tattered and torn
When I look at them
I'm forlorn.

These are my sneakers
I hate them, I do
But in them I could
Outrun you!

Melissa Hawkins

These are my sneakers

Name the possession.

They're both exactly the same
They are old
And very lame.

Complete the quatrain to describe the possession. Lines 2 and 4 rhyme.

These are my sneakers

Repeat the first line.

All tattered and torn
When I look at them
I'm forlorn.

Complete the second quatrain.

These are my sneakers

Repeat the first line one more time.

I hate them, I do
But in them I could
Outrun you!

The last quatrain adds the final touch. It may contain a little humor or an expression of sadness or surprise.

Suggestions

Brainstorm and list some common possessions. Ask students to think about ways the items could be described. Explain that the entire poem should create a word picture filled with colorful details. This makes the use of interesting adjectives very important.

Poetry Patterns • EMC 733

This Is Mine poetry names and describes something you own. It often ends in a funny or surprising way. It follows an ABCB rhyming pattern.

1 Name the thing you own. This will be the first line of your poem.

Line 1: _____

2 On another paper, write phrases to describe the object. Choose the ones you like best. Arrange them so the second line and fourth line of your poem rhyme.

Line 2: _____

Line 3: _____

Line 4: _____

3 Repeat the first line.

Line 5: _____

4 Write more phrases describing the object. Choose the ones you like best. Arrange them so that the sixth line and eighth line of your poem rhyme.

Line 6: _____

Line 7: _____

Line 8: _____

5 Repeat the first line one more time.

Line 9: _____

6 Write the final phrases. Try to use a little humor, an expression of sadness, or a surprising idea. Arrange them so that the tenth line and twelfth line of your poem rhyme.

Line 10: _____

Line 11: _____

Line 12: _____

7 Copy and illustrate your poem.

Poetry Patterns • EMC 733

Metaphor Poetry

Metaphor poetry consists of statements that describe a word in an interesting and imaginative way.

Spring is a warm
sweet hug
from heaven.
Larissa Leavens

School is a station
where little children go
to become little engineers
to guide the world.
Ashley Shields

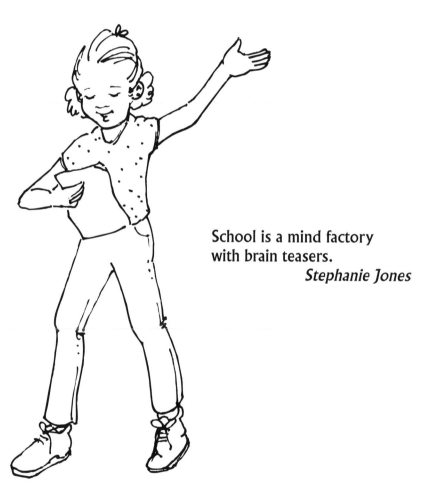

School is a mind factory
with brain teasers.
Stephanie Jones

Suggestions

Share examples of metaphors with your students. Explain that this type of poem relies on the use of imagination. The words in the poem must describe the subject in a unique way, but still be easy to understand.

A **metaphor** poem is a statement that describes
a word in an interesting and imaginative way.

1 Select a subject. It can be a place, a person, an object, an event, or a time of year.

_____

2 List interesting words that describe the subject in a new or unusual way.

_____   _____   _____

_____   _____   _____

_____   _____   _____

3 Choose from your list of words to complete your poem. Arrange the phrases in an
interesting way.

_____

_____

_____

_____

_____

Copy your poem here. Create a border around the poem.

- -

_____
                         title
by _____

_____ is _____

_____

_____

_____

Money Can't Buy Everything Poetry

Money Can't Buy Everything poetry explains in a poetic way what cannot be bought.

Money can't buy everything.
It can't buy a way
To a stony heart.
And it certainly
Can't make a dumb kid smart.
Ryan Rambo

Poetry Patterns • EMC 733

A **Money Can't Buy Everything** poem explains what cannot be bought. The poem may or may not rhyme.

1 Make a list of things that cannot be bought. Select two to write about.

_____ _____ _____

_____ _____ _____

2 Think of interesting words and phrases that describe what it is that cannot be bought. Choose the ones you like best and arrange them in a way that expresses your feelings.

_____

_____

_____

_____

_____

Copy and illustrate your poem here.

Money Can't Buy Everything

by _____

Money can't buy everything.

_____

_____

_____

_____

_____

Poetry Patterns • EMC 733

I Wish Poetry

I **Wish** poetry tells of wanting to be something "impossible" in order to solve one of the world's serious problems.

I wish I were two thousand
miles of wilderness
forbidding
hunting and vehicles,
inviting animals whose
homes have been uprooted by
building, highways, pollution, and people.

Bryan Falk

I wish I were two thousand
miles of wilderness

The "impossible" wish is stated.

forbidding
hunting and vehicles,
inviting animals whose
homes have been uprooted by
building, highways, pollution, and people.

The task that benefits the world (or something in the world) is described.

Suggestions

Brainstorm and list some of the problems of the world that need to be solved. Encourage students to think of the big issues: hunger, prejudice, pollution, war, homelessness, etc. They then use their imaginations to think of what the seemingly "impossible" task would be and the wish they would make.

> **I Wish** poetry tells of wanting to be something "impossible"
> in order to solve one of the world's serious problems.

1 Before starting your poem, you need to decide on two things:
   a. the impossible task you would like to perform
   b. the "wish" that would allow you to complete the task

2 Write your "impossible" wish here.

_____

_____

_____

3 Use your imagination as you describe the task here. Arrange your ideas in an interesting way.

_____

_____

_____

_____

Copy and illustrate your poem here.

- -

I Wish

by _____

I wish I _____

_____

_____

_____

_____

_____

Poetry Patterns • EMC 733

Inside-Outside Poetry

Inside-Outside poetry describes the writer as he or she might be seen by someone. The first stanza focuses on those things the writer doesn't especially like. The following stanza describes the writer as the perfect being of his or her dreams. The poem should rhyme.

My inside self and my outside self
Are different as can be

Begin with an explanation that a difference exists.

My outside self wears dumb clothes
And very short is she.
Dumb freckles sprinkled on her nose
With dumb, short curly hair.
And not pretty at all
With no one to care.

Write a description of the "outside self."

My inside self is different
You can see

Indicate again that there is a difference between the "outside" and "inside" selves.

A lovely ballerina
Dancing inside of me.
Lovely blond hair
Swishing everywhere.
As tall as can be,
Her face is soft,
Her hair so light,
Her feet twinkling
As she dances
Out of sight!
      Julie Jackson

Write a description of the "inside self." Try to end with a flare—a surprise or a bit of humor.

Suggestions

Students think about themselves: the way they look, their abilities, life at school and home, pets, families, dreams for the future, etc. They try to imagine how they appear to others in both negative and positive ways. Encourage students to closely relate the second stanza to the first stanza. For example, if they write about looks in the first stanza, they should write about looks in the second stanza.

The sensitive nature of these poems requires careful consideration about how they are to be shared. Give students the option of keeping their poems private.

Inside-Outside poetry describes you. It tells how you think people see you and how you would like to be seen. It is written in several stanzas using an ABCB rhyming pattern.

First Stanza

1 Begin by writing two lines stating that your "outside self" and "inside self" are different.

_____

_____

2 Write a description of your "outside self" as you think people see you.

_____

_____

_____

_____

Second Stanza

3 Write two lines saying again that there is a difference between your "outside" and "inside" selves.

_____

_____

4 Write a description of your "inside self." This is the time to say all the things you would like to be true about yourself, or the things that are true that people may not notice. Try to end with a surprise or a bit of humor.

_____

_____

_____

_____

5 Check to see that your poem is in an ABCB rhyming pattern.

6 Copy and illustrate your poem.

Poetry Patterns • EMC 733

ABC Poetry

ABC poems do not always make good sense, but they are fun and challenging. The complete alphabet can be used in one poem, or sections of the alphabet can be used in a series of shorter poems.

Start with *A* and go through the alphabet writing a word for each letter. It may be one long poem using the whole alphabet, or a series of shorter poems using part of the alphabet.

A
 Bad
  Cat
   Did
    Eat
     Falling
      Goat
       Hairs
        In
         Jamaica.
Kitten
 Littles
  Make
   Noises
    On
     Pianos.
Questioned
 Raccoons
  Sing
   Tunes
    Under
     Vents
      With
       Xtra
        Yelling
         "Zunes"!
          Mark Johnson

Suggestions

Explain that a good place to begin is to think of a subject, words that describe it, and actions that might occur with it. Then comes the fun part. Manipulate the words to create an alphabetical series that makes some sort of sense. Slang and "made up" words are acceptable in **ABC** poetry.

     Poetry Patterns • EMC 733

ABC poems begin with *A* and go through the alphabet with one word for each letter. Use all the letters for one poem, or write several short poems using sections of the alphabet.

1 Choose a subject. Think of words and phrases that describe it and actions that might happen to it.

_____   _____

_____   _____

_____   _____

_____   _____

2 Start arranging the words and phrases to make sense. Then begin to remove and add other words to create alphabetical order. When you get a series of words you like, write them below.

A _____   N _____

B _____   O _____

C _____   P _____

D _____   Q _____

E _____   R _____

F _____   S _____

G _____   T _____

H _____   U _____

I _____   V _____

J _____   W _____

K _____   X _____

L _____   Y _____

M _____   Z _____

3 Copy and illustrate your poem.

Poetry Patterns • EMC 733

Name Poetry

Name poetry is written in a nonrhyming acrostic form. The letters of a name form the first letter of each line of the poem. Name poetry usually expresses appreciation, interesting insights, or humorous thoughts about the person or object.

Terrific, wonderful teddy bears that
Everybody loves. It scares dark
Dreams away in foggy, starless skies.
Doing nothing but guarding
You from dragons and monstrous sights.

"**B**oy!" what a cuddly sight
Every morning when you awake they
Are lying in dreamland
Right beside your pillow.

Tanya Bulkeley

Suggestions

Name poems can be about a person, pet, object, etc. After selecting a name, students are to think of words and phrases that express their thoughts. Encourage the use of a thesaurus to help students use words that are not too common or overused. In the acrostic form, letters are written vertically and form the first letter of each word or phrase.

> **Name** poetry uses the letters of a name to begin each
> line. The poem may describe the subject, or express
> the writer's thoughts about the subject.

1 Choose a subject. _____

2 List words and phrases that describe the subject or tell how you feel about it.
Choose the ones you like best to use in your poem.

_____   _____

_____   _____

_____   _____

_____   _____

3 Write the letters in the subject's name below. Put one letter on each line. Write a phrase or
sentence after each letter. Change words and phrases until the poem tells what you want it
to say.

_____

_____

_____

_____

_____

_____

_____

_____

_____

4 Copy and illustrate your poem.

Color Poetry

Color poetry describes colors in interesting ways. It can be written in free verse or any familiar rhyming pattern.

Orange is when the sun is setting.
White is new basketball netting.

Grey seems to be a bore.
Blue kites make you want to soar.

Red is as fresh as a rose.
Yellow sun will burn your nose.

Green are the leaves in the spring.
Gold makes a lovely wedding ring.

Pink is baby brother's cheeks.
Purple flowers will bloom in a few weeks.

What are colors to you?
                                    Ryan Crosby

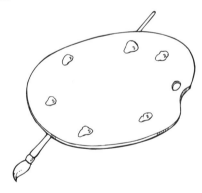

Suggestions

There are many ways to approach **Color** poetry. A color may be represented by one line (Green are the leaves of spring), as a two-line rhyming stanza (What is gray? A foggy day), or as a line of free verse (Blue eyes of a baby make grown men smile). Encourage students to try to make each line special with vivid words, unique ideas, or by organizing the words on the page in an interesting way.

Poetry Patterns • EMC 733

Color poetry describes colors in interesting ways. It can be written in free verse or in your favorite rhyming pattern.

1 Select the colors you want to include in your poem. Write one color in each box. (You don't need to use all of the boxes.)

_____

_____

_____

_____

_____

_____

_____

2 Now you need to decide two things:
Is your poem going to be beautiful, interesting, or funny?
Is it going to rhyme or be free verse?

Write a description after each color in the boxes.

3 Write one final line or couplet making a statement or asking a question about colors.

_____

_____

4 Copy your poem. Make a colorful border around it.

Limericks

A **limerick** is an amusing verse of five lines. Lines 1, 2, and 5 rhyme and lines 3 and 4 rhyme. Line 5 refers back to line 1. Lines 3 and 4 are usually shorter than the other lines.

There once was an alligator named Cicilia
If you ever saw her it would chill ya.
    She wore a hat.
    She was so fat.
She was always trying to kill-ya.
                        Chris Castro

There once was an alligator named Cicilia

The first line almost always begins with "There once was..."

If you ever saw her it would chill ya.

Additional information is told. This line must rhyme with line 1.

She wore a hat.
She was so fat.

Two short, snappy lines that rhyme. These lines give more information about the person, or details about the story.

She was always trying to kill-ya.

Line 5 rhymes with the first two lines. It ends the story or completes the description of the person.

Suggestions

Limericks follow a specific rhythm pattern. Although adherence to a strict rhythm should not be expected, students will get a "feel" for it if you share lots of limericks aloud.

Students need to think of a name (most limericks have a name of a person or place in the first line) and several words that rhyme with it. This will help them determine whether it is possible to use the name in the limerick. It works best to write lines 1, 2, and 5, and then to complete the shorter rhyming couplet that forms lines 3 and 4.

Poetry Patterns • EMC 733

> A **limerick** is a five-line poem that tells a funny or
> silly story. Lines 1, 2, and 5 rhyme. Lines 3 and 4 rhyme
> and are usually shorter than the other lines.

1   Choose the name of the person, place, or thing your limerick is about.

2   Think about your first line. Write it here.

_____

3   Think of a second line. Remember to make it rhyme with line 1. Write it here.

_____

4   Write two short sentences that tell about your topic. Remember, they have to rhyme with each other.

_____

_____

5   Write your final line. It must rhyme with lines 1 and 2. You may want to repeat part of line 1.

_____

Copy and illustrate your poem here.

- -

A Limerick

by_____

_____

_____

_____

_____

_____

    Poetry Patterns • EMC 733

Seasons Poetry

Seasons poetry describes the way a season makes its appearance.

Winter creeps in with
sleigh bells ringing and
birds flying south
on a cold, freezing day
with kids wearing mittens
and snowsuits.

Heather Sack

Winter creeps in with	*The season is named and introduced by an interesting verb.*
sleigh bells ringing and birds flying south	*Two phrases describe what is happening when the season comes.*
on a cold, freezing day	*This phrase tells when the season comes.*
with kids wearing mittens and snowsuits.	*This phrase tells how the season comes.*

Suggestions

After selecting the season, students need to think of interesting ways it might arrive on the scene. It is important to rework the poem until the words make an interesting "picture" in the reader's mind. Phrases such as "creeps in" give more feeling to the poem than "comes in." Encourage students to use a thesaurus to add colorful or more accurate descriptions. This same pattern may be used to write poems about holidays.

Poetry Patterns • EMC 733

Seasons poetry describes the way
a season makes its appearance.

1 Name the season, using an interesting verb to "bring it in."

_____

2 Write two phrases describing what is happening when the season comes.

_____

_____

3 Write a phrase telling when the season comes.

_____

4 Close with one or two phrases telling how the season comes.

_____

_____

Copy and illustrate your poem here.

_____

_____
title

by_____

_____

_____

_____

_____

_____

Poetry Patterns • EMC 733

Clerihew Poetry

A **clerihew** tells about a person in two couplets. The person's name appears in the first line. Traditionally the rhyming pattern is AABB. You may choose to let students select a different rhyming pattern. For example, the sample poem has an ABCB rhyming pattern.

Lincoln's beard was allowed to grow
After a little girl who had no doubt
Wrote a letter and suggested
He'd look better if his whiskers grew out.
Brandy Waldron

Lincoln's beard was allowed to grow
After a little girl who had no doubt

State the name and add a true fact.

Wrote a letter and suggested
He'd look better if his whiskers grew out.

Give additional information to finish this "short story."

Suggestions

Students should choose the name of a person they already know about. They need to write down the ideas and then begin putting the ideas together in a way that tells a little "story." Encourage students to add humor or a strong feeling to the poem.

A **clerihew** tells a little story about a person.
The poem is written in two couplets and must rhyme.

1 Think of a person to be the subject of your poem. It should be someone you know something about. Remember, your poem should tell a little story.

_____

2 List the information you want to include in your poem.

_____

_____

_____

_____

_____

3 Arrange the material into two couplets.
First couplet—State the person's name in the first line. Add a true fact.

_____

_____

4 Second couplet—Give additional information about the person to finish your "short story."

_____

_____

5 Change the words until you are satisfied with the sound of your poem.

6 Copy your poem. Add a drawing of the person you wrote about.

Poetry Patterns • EMC 733

Lonely Poetry

Lonely poetry has two stanzas that tell a short story. The first stanza tells where you are. The second stanza tells what happened. The rhyming pattern is ABCB.

Alone

The first day of June
Alone at home
I watched soap operas
While I let my dog roam.

I heard a screeching noise,
then a dog's bark.
Now I'm very sad.
He's buried in the park.
Jeff Webdell

The first day of June	*This phrase tells when.*
Alone at home	*This phrase expresses lonely feelings.*
I watched soap operas While I let my dog roam.	*These two lines describe what the writer did.*
I heard a screeching noise, then a dog's bark,	*These two lines add more detail to the "story."*
Now I'm very sad. He's buried in the park.	*These last lines provide an ending for the "story."*

Suggestions

Discuss reasons people might feel lonely. Brainstorm phrases that might be used in the second line to express the feeling of loneliness (so sad, all by myself, no one but me, alone I sat, etc.). Send students to the thesaurus to search out other interesting words they might use. Remind them that the poem needs to tell a little story as well as express emotion.

Poetry Patterns • EMC 733

Lonely poetry tells a short story in two stanzas. The
first stanza tells where you are. The second stanza
tells what happened. The rhyming pattern is ABCB.

1 The first line is a phrase that tells when the activity in the poem occurred.

_____

2 The second line expresses lonely feelings.

_____

3 The next two lines describe what you did.

_____

_____

4 The next two lines give more detail about what happened.

_____

_____

5 The last two lines provide the ending to the "story" told in the poem.

_____

_____

6 Adjust the words until you are satisfied with what your poem says. Check your rhyming pattern.

7 Copy and illustrate your poem.

Sneaky Poetry

Sneaky poetry gives interesting clues that "sneak up" to reveal the subject. It is a nonrhyming form that uses interesting or colorful language to describe the poem's subject.

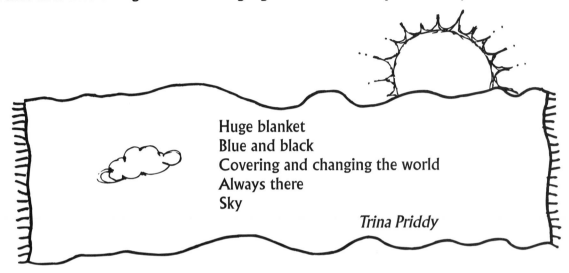

Huge blanket
Blue and black
Covering and changing the world
Always there
Sky

Trina Priddy

Huge blanket	*Think of a noun or phrase that describes or means the same as the subject (listed on the final line of the poem).*
Blue and black	*List adjectives or an adjective and a noun that are related to the subject.*
Covering and changing the world	*List two action words.*
Always there	*Write a thought, phrase, or sentence leading up to the poem's subject.*
Sky	*The subject concludes the poem.*

Suggestions

The first task for students is to decide what two words will form the first and last lines of their poem. These words must be related in an interesting way. For example, chicken and hen are related words, but chicken and egg-layer or chicken and Sunday dinner would make a more interesting poem. Encourage students to build each line in the poem so that it is more like a riddle than a definition.

> **Sneaky** poetry gives interesting clues that "sneak up"
> to reveal your subject. It does not rhyme. It uses interesting
> and colorful language to describe the subject.

1 Think of a place, an object, or a person you want to describe. This word will be the _last_ line of your poem.

List words and phrases that describe the subject in an interesting or colorful way.

_____   _____

_____   _____

_____   _____

_____   _____

2 Arrange words and phrases from your list to complete your poem.
Line 1—Write a noun or phrase that describes or means the same as the subject on the last line.

_____

Line 2—List adjectives or an adjective and a noun that are related to the subject.

_____

Line 3—List two action words describing what the subject might do.

_____

Line 4—Write a thought, phrase, or sentence that leads up to the poem's subject.

_____

Line 5—The subject ends the poem.

_____

3 Copy and illustrate your poem.

Mother's Day Poetry

Mother's Day poetry has five stanzas. Each stanza describes a different feeling or part of the subject's life. It concludes with a special wish or final remark. The rhyme pattern is ABCB.

My mom is really wonderful
She is good to me.
She helps me with my homework
and is as nice as can be.

Mother is introduced and described.

Whatever she does,
She does it right.
When I ask her to help
She can because she's bright.

Describe a part of Mother's life.

I know she gets mad at me
When I don't clean my room.
She goes to the closet
and comes back with the vacuum.

Write about a different part of Mother's life.

She always nags on me
To play with my brother.
She doesn't understand
He's just a bother.

Describe a third part of Mother's life.

My mom she gets real mean
Just like a mother
But that doesn't bother me
'Cause I still love her!

Finish the poem with words of love!

HAPPY MOTHER'S DAY!
Todd Silver

Suggestions

Brainstorm and list the different areas of their mothers' lives about which students might write (family life, work, talents, attitudes, values, goals, dreams, favorite things, humorous traits). Encourage students to use variety in the ideas they choose to express as well as the descriptive language they use.

The same pattern can be used for other people on special days such as Father's Day, Grandparent's Day, or a birthday.

Poetry Patterns • EMC 733

A Mother's Day poem has five stanzas. Each stanza describes a different feeling about your mother, or a different part of her life. It concludes with a special wish or remark. The rhyme pattern is ABCB.

Stanza 1—Introduce and describe your mother.

_____

_____

_____

Stanza 2—Describe a part of your mother's life.

_____

_____

_____

Stanza 3—Write about another part of your mother's life.

_____

_____

_____

Stanza 4—Write about a third part of your mother's life.

_____

_____

_____

Stanza 5—Finish your poem with words of love.

_____

_____

_____

HAPPY MOTHER'S DAY!

Copy and illustrate your poem.

Question Poetry

Question poetry asks questions about the subject. There are usually four questions. The pattern is AABB.

Do trees get tired of standing around all day?
Do they wish they could go out and play?
Do they get tired of birds nesting in their hair?
Do they wish they could sit in a very comfortable chair?
Kevin Mullins

Do trees get tired of standing around all day?   *Imagine that the subject is alive.*

Do they wish they could go out and play?   *Ask sensitive questions.*
Do they get tired of birds nesting in their hair?

Do they wish they could sit in a comfortable chair?   *End with a question that sounds as if you are finished.*

Suggestions

The subject of a question poem can be anything (building, car, plant, animal, etc.) or anyone (friend, parent, hero, character in a book, etc.). The challenge for students is to come up with four questions that give personality to the subject. Encourage students to try to change moods as they write, to add interest to the poem.

Poetry Patterns • EMC 733

Question poetry asks questions about something or someone.
There are usually four questions. The pattern is AABB.

1 Decide on a subject. Think of the kinds of questions you would ask about that person or object.

Question 1:

_____

Question 2:

_____

Question 3:

_____

Question 4:

_____

2 Adjust your wording to fit the rhyming pattern.

Copy and illustrate your poem here.

_____

_____
                    title
by _____

_____

_____

_____

_____

Recipe Poetry

Recipe poetry is an eight-line poem that states a list of items. These items relate to something that is revealed in the last line. The rhyming pattern is ABCB.

> Bathing suits and swimming pools
> Sandals and shorts
> Sweat so hot
> Children playing sports.
> Diving and splashing
> Getting more "dummer."
> "No school. No school."
> This makes summer.
>
> *Stacy Danka*

Bathing suits and swimming pools	*List two items related to the subject. You may describe the items also.*
Sandals and shorts	*List two more items.*
Sweat so hot	*Describe another item.*
Children playing sports.	*Write about an action appropriate to the "recipe." It must rhyme with the second line.*
Diving and splashing	*List two more actions.*
Getting more "dummer."	*Add one more action.*
"No school. No school."	*Try to add something unusual.*
This makes summer.	*Tell what the "recipe" relates to. This line must rhyme with the sixth line.*

Suggestions

Brainstorm and list possible subjects. Encourage students to give free rein to their imaginations. Have them think of everyday things (home and family, things from nature, hobbies and collections) and of funny, serious, or strange things (graduation, peace, sorrow, a mysterious happening). Ask students to think of what elements make up these subjects.

> A **Recipe** poem has eight lines. It names a list of items
> that relate to the last line of your poem.
> The rhyming pattern is ABCB.

1 Decide on a subject. Make a list of items and actions that relate to the subject. Include both nouns and verbs in your list.

_____   _____

_____   _____

_____   _____

_____   _____

2 Use the words and phrases on your list to help write these lines:
(Write your rough draft on another paper.)

Line 1—List two items related to your subject. You may add words to describe the items.

Line 2—List two more items.

Line 3—Describe another item.

Line 4—Write about an action that is appropriate to your "recipe." It must rhyme with line 2.

Line 5—List two more actions.

Line 6—Add one more action.

Line 7—Try to add something unusual that fits with the topic.

Line 8—Name what the recipe "makes." This line must rhyme with line 6.

Check to see that your lines follow the ABCB rhyming pattern.

3 Copy and illustrate your poem.

Tongue Twister Poetry

Tongue Twister poetry is a silly statement in which all words begin with the same sound. The statement should be as long as possible.

Many mummies munch much mush.

Shepherds shear seven shivering shy sheep.
Chris Hupp

Five flying flocks of fleas flew over flapping flags.
Five flapping flags flying up far.
Five flapping flocks of fleas landed on five flying flags.
Five flying flocks of fleas fled from the five flapping flags.
Scott Reames

Suggestions

Invite students to recite any tongue twister they know. Have students identify the sound being used. Was it a simple /s/ or /f/? Or was it a more complicated /sl/ or /fr/? Encourage students to play with many sounds before beginning to write.

Poetry Patterns • EMC 733

Tongue Twister poetry is a silly statement
in which all words begin with the same sound.

1 Select a beginning sound. List as many words as you can beginning with that sound.

_____ _____ _____

_____ _____ _____

_____ _____ _____

2 Write tongue twisters using words from your list. You can write one or several sentences with the same sound. See how long you can make each sentence.

_____

_____

_____

_____

_____

Copy and illustrate your best tongue twister here.

A Tongue Twister

by_____

_____

_____

_____

_____

_____

_____

_____

Poetry Patterns • EMC 733

Comfort Poetry

Comfort poetry contains short, gentle commands given to someone the writer cares about. Comforting words follow the commands.

Shush little girl,
Sleep tonight.
I will be close by,
Sleep tonight.
When you wake up
It will be another day
For exploring
As you play.
Sleep tonight.
                    Fawn Franks

Shush little girl,	*Give a gentle command.*
Sleep tonight.	*Give a second gentle command.*
I will be close by,	*A comforting statement.*
Sleep tonight.	*Repeat line 2.*
When you wake up It will be another day For exploring As you play.	*A little rhyme (a couplet or triplet) giving an explanation, a suggestion, or words of sympathy to make the person feel better.*
Sleep tonight.	*The final line repeats line 2.*

Suggestions

Explain that **Comfort** poetry is written to someone or something in need of tender care. Discuss who or what this might be (someone who is ill, discouraged, sad, or with a serious problem; a young child who has failed in school or in a contest; a pet that is hurt or that must be given away). Have students think of what kind of comfort might be offered.

Poetry Patterns • EMC 733

> **Comfort** poetry contains short, gentle commands given by
> the "speaker" of the poem to someone he or she
> cares about. Comforting words follow the commands.

Decide who is in need of comfort and then follow this pattern.

1 Give a gentle command.

_____

2 Give a second comforting command.

_____

3 Make a comforting statement.

_____

_____

4 Repeat line 2.

_____

5 Write a little rhyme (a couplet or triplet) giving an explanation, a suggestion, or words of sympathy to make the person feel better.

_____

_____

_____

6 Repeat line 2.

_____

7 Copy and illustrate your poem.

I Used To Poetry

I Used To poetry expresses what the writer has learned by comparing the way something used to be with the way it is now. The poem is four lines long. It may follow any rhyming pattern or not rhyme at all.

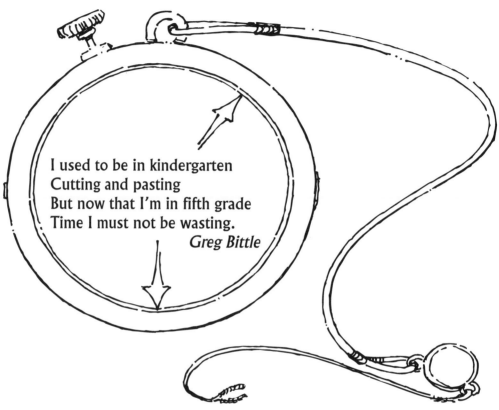

I used to be in kindergarten
Cutting and pasting
But now that I'm in fifth grade
Time I must not be wasting.
                                        Greg Bittle

I used to be in kindergarten
Cutting and pasting

Describe the way it used to be.

But now that I'm in fifth grade
Time I must not be wasting.

Describe the way it is now.

Suggestions

Explain that **I Used To** poems express a lesson that life has taught the writer. Brainstorm and list the places where we learn lessons (home, school, church, in sports, through music, from our friends, etc.). Ask students to think about what they've learned in each of these places. The challenge to writers is stating what has been learned so that it sounds "wise" and not just like an ordinary fact. Since a lot is being said in a short space, students need to choose their words carefully.

Poetry Patterns • EMC 733

An **I Used To** poem tells something you have learned. The poem is four lines long and may follow any rhyming pattern or not rhyme at all.

1 Think of some things you used to do. Where and when did this happen?

_____

_____

_____

_____

2 Choose one thing from your list to write about. In two lines describe the way it used to be.

_____

_____

3 Think about how this has changed for you. Write two new lines to describe how it is now.

_____

_____

Copy your poem below.

Then and Now

by_____

I used to _____

_____

But now _____

_____

Trouble Poetry

Trouble poetry contains two ideas written in couplet form. The first line states the trouble. The second line gives a humorous, unusual, or clever explanation or conclusion.

The trouble with soda pop is that
Eventually it becomes flat.
Andy Stanley

The trouble with soda pop is that   *The trouble is stated.*

Eventually it becomes flat.   *An explanation is given.*

Suggestions

Encourage students to think about what the "trouble" might be with ordinary things they see or use every day.

Poetry Patterns • EMC 733

Trouble poetry is two ideas long. The first idea states the trouble. The second idea explains why it is trouble.

1 Think of some ordinary things. What could be the trouble with these items? See how many interesting ideas you can come up with.

_____

_____

_____

_____

_____

2 Select one of your ideas. Write two rhyming lines about it.

Line 1—State the trouble.

_____

_____

Line 2—Explain why it is trouble.

_____

_____

Copy and illustrate your poem below.

- -

Trouble

by _____

_____

_____

_____

_____

Walking Poetry

Walking poetry tells of going somewhere. It describes the scene and expresses the author's feelings about it. The rhyming pattern is ABCB.

We took a walk the other day
Just me and my friend Todd.
We walked by an old house.
My it was odd.

These lines tell who went on the walk and where they walked.

We saw a cat we frightened.
We looked at the dead old trees.
We saw half a broken fence.
We felt the bitter cool breeze.

These lines describe what was seen.

I like the places that we go.
I like to peek and peer
But this is very spooky
So let's get outta here!
                    Russell Randel

These lines tell how the "walker" felt.

Suggestions

This pattern can be used for any type of "moving" activity (swimming, hiking, diving, exploring, etc.). Encourage students to try to create a mood (happiness, sadness, fear, excitement, etc.).

Poetry Patterns • EMC 733

Walking poetry tells about going somewhere. It describes the scene and expresses your feelings about it. The rhyming pattern is ABCB.

1 Think about who went on the walk, where they walked, and what they saw. (One of the people can be you, but doesn't have to be.) You might want to try out several ideas before you start your poem.

2 In four lines, describe who went on the walk and where they walked.

_____

_____

_____

_____

3 In four lines, describe what was seen.

_____

_____

_____

_____

4 In four lines, describe how the "walker" felt.

_____

_____

_____

_____

5 Check your rhyming pattern. In each stanza, lines 2 and 4 must rhyme.

6 Copy and illustrate your poem.

Subject Poetry

Subject poems are acrostic poems. The letters of the subject are used to start each line. The subject word is written vertically, and a word or phrase about the subject is written after each letter.

Star

Stars are bright
   and beautiful
Together they glisten and
   shine like glitter.
A star is a light
   bright in the night so
Reach for the stars and
   fight through the night.
Karee Richardson

Horses

How they gallop—lovely!
One foot at a time.
Rustling the grass so softly.
Sun beating down on dapple grey backs,
Easily scared at a touch!
So beautiful and graceful!
Addie Turner

Suggestions

Students need to be careful in the selection of a subject word. Long words are more difficult to use than short words. Words containing infrequently used letters such as *x* or *z* are more difficult to use than words with commonly used letters.

Encourage students to get an idea about what they want to say first, and then adjust words (change, add, omit) to fit the letters in the subject. Without some planning the poem will not make sense.

Poetry Patterns • EMC 733

> **Subject** poems are written using the
> letters of the subject to start each line.

1 Choose a subject. Make a list of words that tell about the subject. The words should all begin with one of the letters in the word you choose. (You may need to use a dictionary or thesaurus.)

_____   _____   _____

_____   _____   _____

_____   _____   _____

_____   _____   _____

_____   _____   _____

_____   _____   _____

_____   _____   _____

_____   _____   _____

2 Write your word _vertically_ with one letter on each line. Choose words or phrases that have a pleasing or interesting sound. Remember, each word or phrase must begin with a letter in the topic word. The poem should make sense.

_____

_____

_____

_____

_____

3 Copy and illustrate your poem.

Poetry Patterns • EMC 733

People Poetry

People poetry tells about a person's character, talent, or accomplishments.

Jackie Joyner Kersey
For the stars and stripes
Rapidly racing
Faster than the speed of light
If only I were like her!
Rebecca Simonian

Jackie Joyner Kersey — *Name the person who is the subject of the poem.*

For the stars and stripes — *Give a description using words connected by "and" or "but."*

Rapidly racing — *Use an adverb ("-ly" word) and a verb to describe a typical action.*

Faster than the speed of light — *Compare a quality using "as a" or "than."*

If only I were like her! — *Close with a wish for the person or yourself, using "If only," "I wish," "I'll never," or "I always."*

Suggestions

Brainstorm and list people who might be subjects for a poem. These can be people selected from current events, history, or the writer's own life. Remind students to select someone they know facts about. They are to write about the person's talent or character, or about something the person has done.

A **People** poem tells about a
person in five nonrhyming lines.

1 Think about a person you find interesting. It can be a person you know, a person from history, or a person in the news today. Write down a few things you know about the character, talents, or actions of the person.

_____

_____

_____

_____

_____

2 Use what you know about the person to complete your poem.

Line 1—Write the name of the person.

_____

Line 2—Write a description using two words connected by "and" or "but."

_____

Line 3—Use an adverb and a verb to describe a typical action.

_____

Line 4—Compare a quality of the person with something interesting using "as a" or "than."

_____

Line 5—Close with a wish for the person or yourself, using "If only," "I wish," "I'll never," or "always."

_____

3 Copy and illustrate your poem.

Simile Poetry

Simile poetry uses "as" or "like" to compare the subject to something else.

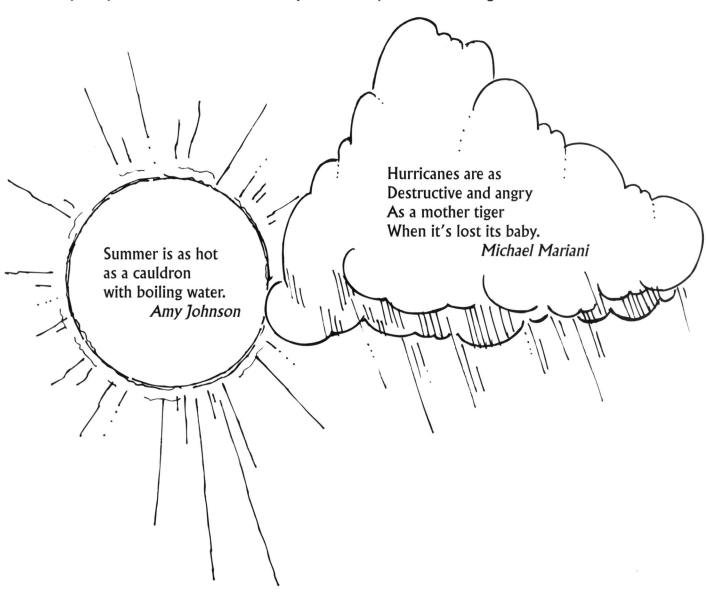

Summer is as hot
as a cauldron
with boiling water.
Amy Johnson

Hurricanes are as
Destructive and angry
As a mother tiger
When it's lost its baby.
Michael Mariani

Suggestions

Share some similes with your class. Use examples having both "as" and "like."Before students begin to write, suggest some subjects and have students think of similes that can be made. (For example, "The explosion was like a 7.0 earthquake"; "My mother's touch is as gentle as a soft breeze.") Explain that a good **Simile** poem creates an interesting or exciting picture in the reader's mind.

> **Simile** poetry uses "as" or "like" to compare the subject to something else.

1 Think of a subject. _____

2 List words and phrases that can be compared to the subject.

_____   _____

_____   _____

_____   _____

3 Try several descriptive statements.

_____ is as: _____
subject
                           _____

                           _____

_____ is like: _____
subject
                             _____

                             _____

Choose the simile you like best and write it below. Make a border around it.

- -

_____
                    title
by_____

_____ is _____

_____

Seven Poetry

Seven poetry is a rhyme about what happened to the seven things in a group. The poems are meant to be humorous and maybe a little crazy!

There were seven sisters
Sleeping in a bed.
The first fell off
And bumped her head.
The second cried all through the night.
The third was loudly snoring.
And the fourth wanted a night light.
The fifth wanted Mommy,
The sixth wanted Dad.
The seventh rolled all around
And made everyone mad.
                    Kim Hanscom

There were seven sisters	*Name the group of seven.*
Sleeping in a bed.	*Tell what they were doing.*
The first fell off And bumped her head.	*Use two lines to describe what happened to the first member of the group.*
The second cried all through the night. The third was loudly snoring. And the fourth wanted a night light. The fifth wanted Mommy, The sixth wanted Dad.	*Describe the next five members of the group in one line each.*
The seventh rolled all around And made everyone mad.	*To conclude the poem, describe the last member of the group in two lines.*

Suggestions

Brainstorm and list possible groups of seven (ball players, animals, taxi drivers, dancers, babies, clowns, etc.). Discuss what the group might be doing. Encourage students to use their imaginations as they think of unusual things their group might do.

Poetry Patterns • EMC 733

Seven poetry is a funny rhyme about the
actions of a group of seven listed one by one.

Think about a group of seven people or animals that belong together in some way. Think about
seven things this group might do. Complete the sentences describing what is happening.

1 Name the group of seven.

There were _____ .

2 Tell what they are doing.

_____ .

3 Use two lines to describe what happened to the first member of the group.

The first one _____ .

4 Describe what happened to the next five members of the group in one line each.

The second one _____ .

The third one _____ .

The fourth one _____ .

The fifth one _____ .

The sixth one _____ .

5 End the poem with two lines about the last member of the group.

The seventh one _____ .

6 Copy and illustrate your poem.

Poetry Patterns • EMC 733

Bio Poetry

Bio poetry gives basic information about a person in a poetic form following a specific pattern.

Becky	*Name the person.*
Loving, Trustworthy, Loyal,	*Give three adjectives that describe the person.*
Wishes to fly like a bird,	*Tell what the person wishes to do.*
Dreams of making peace in the world,	*Tell what the person dreams of.*
Wants to heal the sick and poor.	*Tell what the person wants to do.*
Who wonders what lies beyond the stars.	*Tell what the person wonders about.*

Poetry Patterns • EMC 733

Who fears war. Who is afraid of famine.	*Tell what the person fears.*
Who likes boys with blond, wavy hair.	*Tell what the person likes.*
Who believes in God.	*Tell what the person believes.*
Who loves rice and fortune cookies. Who loves to play volleyball. Who loves school, especially math. Who loves soft tacos with only meat and cheese.	*Tell what the person loves.*
Who plans to be a missionary. Who plans to be a faithful wife. Who plans to live the good life.	*Tell what the person plans to do.*
Whose final destination is heaven. *Becky Jaspar*	*Add a closing line.*

Suggestions

While any person can be the subject of this poetry pattern, it is important that the writer know the subject very well. Ask students to think of people they know enough about to use as a subject (parent, sibling, best friend). The easiest person to write about is oneself. Students need to look carefully at each step as they write. Some directions are very specific (e.g., "Write three adjectives"). At other times a direction is given, but no specific number is stated (e.g., "Tell what the person plans to do"). In that case, the writer may include more than one line. Encourage students to think about interesting language as well as giving facts.

> **Bio** poetry gives basic information about a person
> (yourself or someone you know very well)
> in a poetic form, following a specific pattern.

1 Decide who you are going to write about. Then follow the pattern to complete your poem.

2 _____

person's name

3 _____ , _____ , _____

three adjectives that describe the person

4 Write one or more lines beginning with each of these phrases:

Wishes to _____

_____

_____

Dreams of _____

_____

_____

Wants to _____

_____

_____

Who wonders _____

_____

_____

Who fears _____

_____

_____

Who likes _____

_____

_____

Who believes _____

_____

_____

Who loves _____

_____

_____

Who plans _____

_____

_____

5 Add a closing line.

_____

6 Copy and illustrate your poem.

Sharing Student-Authored Poetry

Provide opportunities for students to share their poems with others. This modeling will motivate continued writing and will be especially helpful for hesitant writers.

Display Boards

If you plan to do a great deal of writing during the school year, you may want to set aside one bulletin board area just for displaying your students' original writings.

Cover a bulletin board with butcher paper. Add a heading cut from colorful construction paper. Mount poems on construction paper. Pin poems to the board. Change the poems frequently.

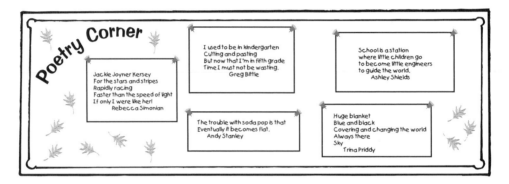

Charts and Banners

Students copy and illustrate an original poem on banners or charts. Hang the banners or charts on a bulletin board or a chart rack so that students can share each other's work.

An easy banner can be made using 12" x 24" (30.5 x 61 cm) butcher paper and a 30" (76 cm) piece of yarn. Fold the top of the paper under twice, about 1" (2.5 cm) each time. Place the yarn under the fold and glue the fold down. Tie the ends of the yarn together. Write the poem on the banner using marking pens.

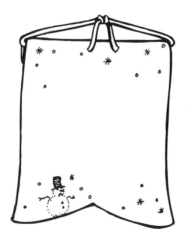 

Poetry Patterns • EMC 733

Newsletter

Once a month (quarter, semester, etc.), send home a newsletter containing students' original poetry created during that period. Have students design a newsletter format. It should include the newsletter's title, issue number, and date.

Program

Invite parents and other interested parties to a program where students recite their own (or classmates') poetry. Assign students to design an invitation and a program.

Planning a program doesn't need to be a complicated process. Students sitting in groups on the stage floor or on stools can be as effective as elaborate staging and costumes. Punch and cookies afterwards gives everyone a chance to get better acquainted (and to pass around compliments to your class poets).

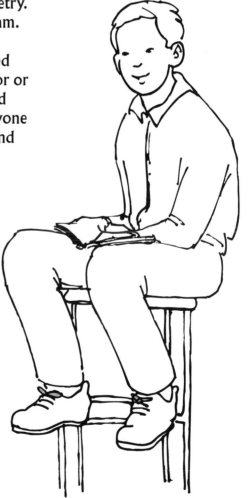

Collecting Student-Authored Poems

Portfolios

Use an art period near the beginning of the school year to create individual portfolios in which to save original poetry. These can be as simple as large manila envelopes decorated with marking pens or crayons. They may be elaborate portfolios made from butcher paper or tagboard decorated with collages or block printing and tied with yarn or ribbon.

As the year progresses, students save their poetry in their portfolios. When you are ready to create newsletters or class books, students will have a nice selection from which to choose. It is exciting for students to see how much their writing improves over a period of time.

Poetry Books

Putting books written and illustrated by your students into a class library is an excellent way to collect and to share students' original poetry. Follow these steps for putting a book together:

1. Create pages.

2. Attach poem pages.
   Pages may be stapled together before being put into a cover.

   Pages may be glued to a backing of construction paper, and then stapled together and put into a cover.

   Pages may be folded in half, and then glued back-to-back.

   Pages may be folded, and then stitched down the center. Stitching may be done by machine or by hand with darning needles.

3. Create covers (see page 95).

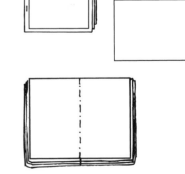

Book-Binding Techniques

Covers can be made from many different materials.

mat board	cardboard
construction paper	wallpaper
tagboard	cloth

- **Hinged Cover**

Cut two pieces of cover material slightly larger than the poetry pages.

Cut 1/2" (1.25 cm) strip from the left-hand side of the front cover.

Tape the strips together on the inside. Leave a small space open between the two strips.

Staple the cover and poetry pages together. Cover the front hinge and staples and the back staples with a 1 1/2" (3.75 cm) strip of tape.

- **Cloth Cover**

Cut two pieces of cardboard slightly larger than the story pages.

Place the cardboard on a piece of cloth about 1 to 1 1/2" (2.5–3.75 cm) larger than the cover. Leave a small space in between the cover pieces.

Miter the corners.

Place diluted white glue on the cloth and fold over the cover.

Paper should be cut almost the length of the cover. Stitch 6 or 8 pages together down the center with a darning needle and thread or use a sewing machine.

Leave the first and last pages empty to serve as end papers. Copy and illustrate original poems on the pages. Paste the end papers to the cover to complete the book.

Bibliography

A Bad Case of Giggles: Kids' Favorite Funny Poems by Bruce Lansky; Meadowbrook, 1994.

A Light in the Attic by Shel Silverstein; HarperCollins, 1981.

A. Nonny Mouse Writes Again! edited by Jack Prelutsky; Dragonfly, 1996.

Antarctic Antics: A Book of Penguin Poems by Judy Sierra; Harcourt Brace, 1998.

At the Crack of the Bat: Baseball Poems designed by Lillian Morrison; Hyperion Press, 1992.

Beast Feast by Douglas Florian; Harcourt Brace, 1994.

The Beauty of the Beast: Poems from the Animal Kingdom edited by Jack Prelutsky; Knopf, 1997.

The Block: Poems by Langston Hughes; Viking Children's Books, 1995.

Call Down the Moon: Poems of Music edited by Myra Cohn Livingston; Margaret McElderry, 1995.

Calling the Doves/El canto de las palomas by Juan Felipe Herrera; Childrens Book Press, 1995.

Cricket Never Does: A Collection of Haiku and Tanka by Myra Cohn Livingston; Margaret McElderry, 1997.

Daffy Down Dillies: Silly Limericks by Edward Lear; Boyds Mill Press, 1992.

The Earth Is Painted Green: A Garden of Poems about Our Planet edited by Barbara Brenner; Scholastic Trade, 1994.

Falling Up: Poems and Drawings by Shel Silverstein; HarperCollins, 1996.

Hailstones and Halibut Bones: Adventures in Color by Mary O'Neil; Doubleday, 1989.

Hiawatha by Henry Wadsworth Longfellow; Puffin, 1996.

Hiawatha's Childhood by Henry Wadsworth Longfellow; Farrar, Straus & Giroux, 1984.

In the Eyes of the Cat: Japanese Poetry for All Seasons by Demi; Henry Holt, 1994.

I, Too, Sing America: Three Centuries of African American Poetry edited by Catherine Clinton; Clarion Books, 1998.

Knock at a Star by X. M. Kennedy & Dorothy M. Kennedy; Little, Brown & Company, 1985.

The New Kid on the Block by Jack Prelutsky; Greenwillow, 1994.

The Oxford Book of Children's Verse in America edited by Donald Hall; Oxford University Press, 1990.

Paul Revere's Ride by Henry Wadsworth Longfellow; Puffin, 1996.

Poems Have Roots by Lillian Moore; Atheneum, 1997.

Ring of Earth by Jane Yolen; Harcourt Brace, 1986.

Spring: A Haiku Story by George Shannon; Greenwillow, 1996.

Stopping By Woods on a Snowy Evening by Robert Frost; Puffin, 1998.

This Same Sky: A Collection of Poems from Around the World compiled by Naomi Shihab Nye; Simon and Schuster, 1992.